Quiz
145912

W9-BFZ-225

Published in 2012 by The Rosen Publishing Group, Inc.
29 East 21st Street, New York, NY 10010

First Edition

Editor: Joanne Randolph
Book Design: Planman Technologies
Illustrations: Planman Technologies

Library of Congress Cataloging-in-Publication Data

Smith, Andrea P.
Casey Jones / by Andrea P. Smith. — 1st ed.
    p. cm. — (Jr. graphic American legends)
Includes bibliographical references and index.
ISBN 978-1-4488-5195-9 (library binding) — ISBN 978-1-4488-5228-4 (pbk.) —
ISBN 978-1-4488-5229-1 (6-pack)
1. Jones, Casey, 1863-1900—Juvenile literature. 2. Locomotive engineers—
United States—Biography—Juvenile literature. I. Title. II. Series.
TF140.J6S65 2012
385'.36092—dc22
[B]
                                                              2011001712

Manufactured in the United States of America

CPSIA Compliance Information: Batch #PLS1102PK: For Further Information contact Rosen Publishing, New York,
New York at 1-800-237-9932

Contents

Main Characters

Casey Jones (1863–1900) Born John Luther Jones and given the nickname Casey. He was the railroad **engineer** on the "**Cannonball** Express," a passenger train that collided with a stalled freight train on April 30, 1900. He died trying to save the train and all the passengers on board.

Mary Joanna "Janie" Jones (1866–1958) She married Casey Jones in 1886 and was the mother of their three children.

Wallace Saunders (c. late 1800s–early 1900s) One of Casey Jones's railroad friends. He composed and sang the ballad that made Casey Jones famous.

Simeon T. Webb (1874–1957) A railroad **fireman** who worked with Casey Jones. He was working with Jones on the night that Jones died.

CASEY JONES

IN 1876, WHEN CASEY WAS A BOY, THE JONES FAMILY MOVED FROM MISSOURI TO KENTUCKY. ALL THE BOYS IN THE FAMILY WERE **FASCINATED** BY TRAINS.

JOHN, LATER NICKNAMED CASEY, LOVED TALKING TO THE MEN WORKING ON THE TRAINS.

ONE DAY, I'LL BE THE ENGINEER ON THAT TRAIN.

JOHN MOVED TO A BOARDINGHOUSE OWNED BY THE BRADY FAMILY AND QUICKLY FELL IN LOVE WITH JANIE BRADY, WHO HELPED HER PARENTS AND SERVED MEALS.

WHERE ARE YOU FROM?

CAYCE, KENTUCKY.

YOU NEED A NICKNAME. WE'LL CALL YOU CASEY.

JANIE, I AM SO HAPPY YOU MARRIED ME. WE'LL MAKE OUR HOME RIGHT HERE IN TENNESSEE.

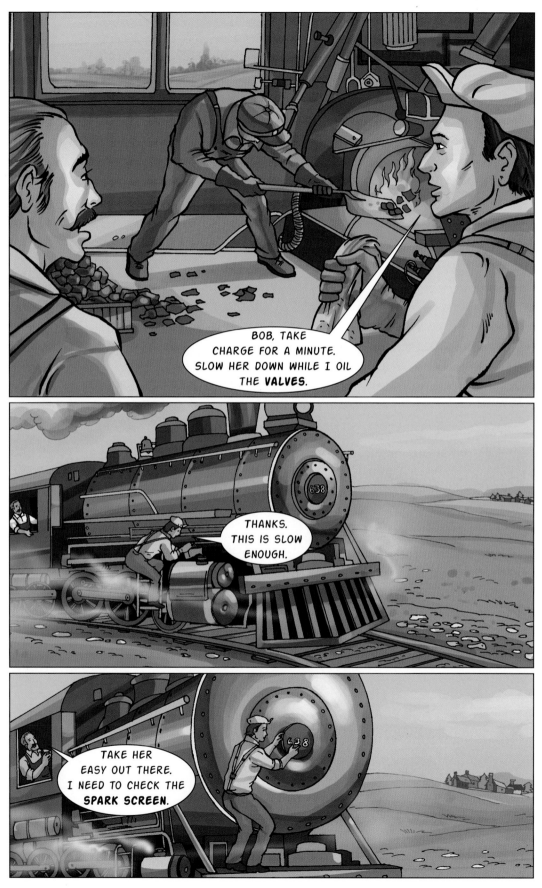

WE BETTER GET THESE FREIGHT TRAINS OUT OF THE WAY. THE CANNONBALL IS COMING THROUGH.

THE TRAIN'S STUCK. THERE'S NO WAY TO CLEAR THE TRACKS.

I'VE GOT TO STOP THIS TRAIN.

THE LEGEND CONTINUED WITH THE PUBLICATION OF *CASEY JONES: EPIC OF THE AMERICAN RAILROAD* AND A RADIO SERIES.

CASEY'S HEROIC ACTIONS INSPIRED A TV SERIES "CASEY JONES: THE LEGEND." HIS HOME IS NOW A MUSEUM.

TODAY, THE LEGEND LIVES ON AT THE CASEY JONES VILLAGE IN JACKSON, TENNESSEE.

Timeline

March 4, 1863   John Luther Jones is born in Missouri.

1876   The Jones family moves to Cayce, Kentucky.

1878   John, later nicknamed Casey, leaves home to become a railroad man.

November 25, 1886   Casey Jones marries Janie Brady.

March 1, 1888   Jones becomes fireman for Illinois Central (I.C.) Railroad.

February 23, 1891   Jones is promoted to engineer on I.C. freight trains.

1893   Jones is engineer on passenger service at Chicago's World Fair.

c. 1895   Jones rescues a young girl from the train tracks.

April 30, 1900   Casey Jones dies while trying to stop the train he is driving, saving all passengers on board.

1902(?)   Wallace Saunders writes a ballad about Casey Jones.

1909   Songwriting team Siebert and Newton copyright a song about Casey's heroic actions.

1927   The movie *Casey Jones* is released.

1939   *Casey Jones: Epic of the American Railroad* is published.

1950   The U.S. Postal Service releases a commemorative postal stamp.

1956   Casey Jones's home opens as museum.

1957   Sim Webb, fireman saved by Casey's shout for him to jump from the train, dies.

1958   A television series "Casey Jones" stars Alan Hale, Jr.

Glossary

brakeman (BRAYK–man) The person on the railroad crew who helps the engineer and the conductor.

cannonball (KA-nun-bawl) A fast-moving train.

engineer (en-juh-NEER) The person who drives the railroad engine.

fascinated (FA-sin-ayt-ed) Very interested.

fireman (FYR-man) Someone who shovels coal into the hot stove of the engine, which makes steam and powers the train.

locomotive (loh-kuh-MOH-tiv) The first train car, which pulls the rest of the cars.

marvel (MAR-vul) A wonderful or great thing.

passenger (PA-sin-jur) A person who rides in or on a moving thing.

spark screen (SPAHRK-SKREEN) A part made of metal mesh that stopped sparks from flying out of a steam or coal-powered train engine.

survived (sur-VYVD) Continued to exist.

telegrams (TEL-uh-gramz) Messages sent by telegraphs, machines used to send messages through wires using coded signals.

throttle (THRAH-tul) A handle that controls the supply of fuel to an engine.

valves (VALVZ) Parts that control the flow of water or other matter.

Index

Web Sites

Due to the changing nature of Internet links, Power Kids Press has developed an online list of Web sites related to the subject of this book. This site is updated regularly. Please use this link to access the list:

www.powerkidslinks.com/JGAM/jones